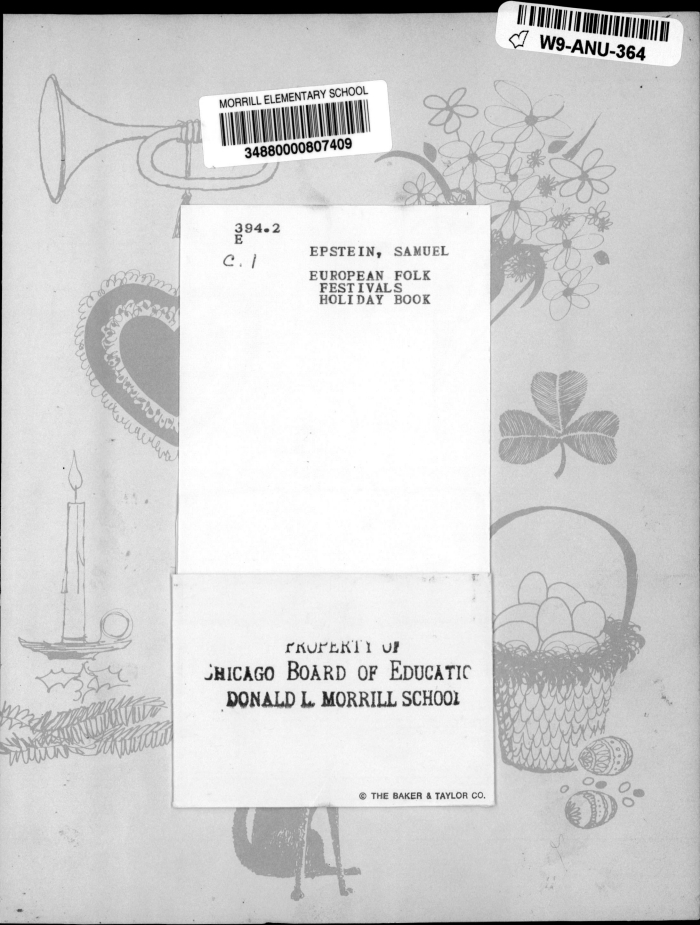

394.2
E

C. 1

EPSTEIN, SAMUEL

EUROPEAN FOLK
FESTIVALS
HOLIDAY BOOK

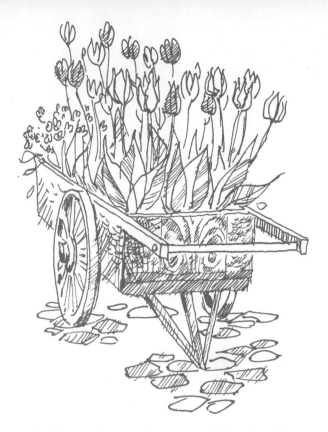

A HOLIDAY BOOK
European Folk Festivals

BY SAM AND BERYL EPSTEIN

ILLUSTRATED BY JOSEPH A. SMITH

GARRARD PUBLISHING COMPANY
CHAMPAIGN, ILLINOIS

Holiday books are edited under
the educational supervision of

Charles E. Johnson, Ed. D.
Professor of Education
University of Georgia

Contents

1 May Day

In the merry month of May . . .

Beasts did leap, and birds did sing,

Trees did grow and plants did spring . . .
— *Richard Barnfield*

It is almost three o'clock on the afternoon of April 30th, the eve of May Day. Hundreds of students stand in front of the library of Uppsala University, in Sweden. Hidden in their pockets are white velvet student caps.

The students have not worn their caps all winter long. When they put them on it will mean, "Spring is here!"

The head of the university, called the rector, stands on a balcony above the crowd. He holds a watch in his hand. He too has a cap hidden in his pocket.

At exactly three o'clock the rector pulls out his cap. He lifts it high over his head.

This is the signal the students are waiting for. Suddenly they are all waving their caps wildly in the air. Then they put them on and give three loud cheers for spring.

Now they all turn around. They face the broad avenue that leads downhill to the town square. They form lines and link arms. They start running down the hill as fast as they can go.

When the first lines reach the square, they turn and start back up the hill. They collide with the boys and girls still trying to reach the square. A "battle" begins.

Students push and shove one another.

Each group tries to force the other out of its way. But everybody is laughing. Neither group wins or loses.

Some historians say that the students are acting out the age-old battle between winter and spring. The students say that they are just having a good time.

That evening they hold the biggest parties of their school year. They dance all night. All-night parties are held at other Swedish universities too. The young people do not want to go to bed until they have seen the dawn of May Day.

May Day is more important in northern Europe than in the warmer countries farther south. Winter in the north is long and cold and dark. People grow tired of snow and ice and short winter days. May Day means that spring has come at last. Everyone wants to celebrate.

Some May Day celebrations began many centuries ago in pagan times. People then did not understand what caused the change of seasons. When winter came, they thought that evil spirits had captured the sun and put him in prison. As long as he remained there, the earth would be cold and dark.

May Day was said to be the day when the sun tried to escape. To help him, people lit big bonfires on the hilltops. They believed that the fires frightened away the evil spirits who tried to keep the sun prisoner.

Later, in the Middle Ages, people believed in witches. They said these evil creatures met every May Day on the Brocken. The Brocken is a high peak in the Harz Mountains of Germany. The witches flew there on their broomsticks. On their way they swooped down on people to harm them.

Huge fires were built to frighten the witches away. Then people prayed to Saint Walpurga. They believed that this eighth-century saint could protect them from the witches. May Day Eve was called Walpurgis Night in her honor.

Today few people believe in witches or evil spirits. But in Denmark, Norway, and Sweden people still build fires on Walpurgis Night. In villages in the Harz Mountains, people parade through the streets. They carry ugly straw witches. Later they burn the ugly figures in memory of Saint Walpurga.

In some countries, May Day is more important than May Day Eve. In Belgium some towns welcome spring that day with parades and fairs. In eastern Switzerland people offer up special May Day prayers for good crops.

In northern France, on May Day, people
pick lilies of the valley in the woods. If
they live in Paris, and cannot easily go to
the woods, they buy the flowers at sidewalk
stands. They wear them and give them to
their friends for luck.

May Day has always been a popular children's holiday in England. Boys and girls gather around a maypole set up on a village green. They crown a girl Queen of the May. Sometimes they crown a boy as May King. Then they all dance around the maypole.

Grownups often take part in May Day dancing too. They perform the old traditional folk dances called Morris dances. In some towns, men form teams of dancers called "Morris men." They wear broad sashes across their chests. Their hats are decorated with ribbons and flowers and bells. Crowds follow them as they dance up one street and down another.

Another old English custom is "singing in the May." Two places are famous for it—Oxford University, and the town of Southampton.

At Oxford, early on May Day, a student choir sings from the top of a high tower. Hundreds of students gather below to listen. Some stand on a bridge over the river that flows past the tower. Others sit in small, flat boats, called punts, floating on the river.

Bells ring out as the last song ends. This is the signal for "punt scuttling." Students in the punts push each other's boats with long poles. They try to upset them.

Splash! The first punt tips over. Students shout as they land in the chilly water and wade to shore.

Splash! Another punt goes over, and then another. Those watching from the shore laugh and cheer.

Finally all the boats have been tipped over and the "scuttlers" are dripping wet.

Oxford's telephone wake-up service is always busy on May Day morning. Hundreds of people have asked to be wakened with a call. They do not want to miss the fun.

The custom of "singing in the May" at Southampton was given up during the first World War. Then people decided to bring it back again. In 1957, they asked a boys' school choir to sing on May Day morning.

The boys sang at six o'clock in the town square. They stood under an archway that had been a gate in the old city wall. Only a few people came out to hear them.

"We wish the boys would sing later in the morning, when more of us are awake," many people said.

The next year the boys sang at eight o'clock. A big crowd gathered to listen.

16

That made other people complain. They said, "We couldn't push through the crowd and get to work on time. The boys should sing even later—or much earlier."

Then the British Broadcasting Company decided to put the boys on television. The BBC wanted them to sing at ten o'clock. Some people complained about that hour too!

Southampton learned that it is not easy to bring an old custom back to life. Yet most people are glad that this one is alive again. Now all England can hear the boys of Southampton sing a welcome to May Day and spring.

2 Whitsuntide Festivals

Whitsuntide is a special week in the spring. It starts on the day known as Whitsunday, or the Pentecost, seven weeks after Easter.

Jews celebrated the Pentecost in Palestine long before the time of Jesus Christ. It was called the Festival of Harvest and the Festival of First Fruits. It marked the end of the grain harvest in that warm Mediterranean land.

Christians began to celebrate the Pentecost for another reason. The Bible says that Christ's disciples received "the gift of tongues" on that day. This means they were suddenly able to speak many languages. Then they could preach Christ's teachings to the whole world. Christians say that the Pentecost is the birthday of their church.

New Christians were often baptized on the Pentecost. They wore white robes during the ceremony. Those white robes gave the holiday its English name of White Sunday, or Whitsunday.

Today Whitsunday is celebrated in many ways. People decorate their churches and cathedrals with spring flowers. In some German and Swiss towns, people march to church in long, solemn processions. Some Portuguese church societies cook and serve meals for the poor.

Other Whitsuntide celebrations are gay festivals that have nothing to do with religion. The fields and gardens of Europe are usually full of flowers at this time of the year. People celebrate the growing things of spring.

In Denmark and Norway, in Sweden and France, families go out into the country on picnics. They sing and dance in the fields.

They cut green branches and take them home to decorate their houses.

In the Black Forest in Germany, shepherds buy new bells for their sheep on Whitsunday. They try the bells out before they buy them. Each man wants to be sure that all the bells for his herd sound well together. All day the sound of ringing bells echoes through the forest.

In Zaandam, and other towns in the Netherlands, the day before Whitsunday has a special name. It is called *Luilak*, or Lazybones Day. Before dawn young people rush into the streets to make noise.

They beat on pots and pans. They shout. They whistle. They blow horns. They ring doorbells and pound on doors.

They are trying to wake everybody up.

If one of their friends continues to sleep, they stand under his window and shout:

Lazybones, tucked in his bed,
Gets up at nine o'clock!
Nine o'clock, half-past nine—
Then you can see Lazybones.

When the Lazybones finally appears, he has to buy candy or cakes for his friends. Bakeries make special Lazybone cakes.

A beautiful Lazybones festival takes place in Haarlem's famous flower market. Haarlem is a big city in the Netherlands.

Flower merchants arrive in the big market square early the evening before. They arrange their flowers on tables and carts. There are red and white tulips, yellow daffodils, blue irises, and red geraniums. When all the flowers have been arranged, the lights in the square are turned off.

Soon the dark square fills with people. At midnight, church bells ring out. At the same time, big floodlights go on. As if by magic, the thousands of flowers appear.

The festival goes on until dawn. Hand organs play and the young people dance. Food stands are set up. Many sell small herrings, the favorite fish of Netherlanders. And people stroll about with armfuls of flowers they have bought for Whitsunday.

Whitmonday is the day after Whitsunday. Young girls in Ecaussines, Belgium, give a special party on that day. They call it a Matrimonial Tea Party. They invite all the bachelors of the neighborhood.

Streets are decorated with streamers and flowers. Hundreds of bachelors, young and old, parade to the party two by two. The girls serve them tea and cakes, and tease them about not being married. Afterward they all dance at a big open-air ball.

In the English village of Cooper's Hill, people hold a cheese-chasing festival on Whitmonday. That afternoon boys and girls climb to the top of Cooper's Hill. There, a man in a white smock and a tall silk hat stands guard over a big round cheese. It is packed safely inside a round wooden case.

At six o'clock the man gives the case a hard shove. It starts rolling down the

grassy slope. The boys and girls chase after
it. Faster and faster goes the cheese, zig-
zagging like a frightened rabbit. The
children zig-zag too. The one who finally
catches the cheese wins it for a prize.

Whitsuntide fairs take place in many English towns. One of the most famous is the Ram Roasting Fair at Kingsteignton on Whit-Tuesday.

Schools are closed and the whole town gathers to watch the roasting of a big ram. It is turned slowly on a spit over a log fire. While it roasts, a little girl is chosen queen

of the fair. School teams run races. There is a horse show too. Stands sell ice cream, sausages, and tarts.

When the ram is done, everyone wants to taste it. There is never enough to go around. Slices are auctioned off to the highest bidders. The money goes to the poor and the sick of the town.

Kingsteignton's ram roasting is hundreds of years old. One legend says it started after a long drought. A farmer asked a witch how he could get water for his cattle and crops.

She told him to kill a large ram in a dry stream bed. She said that would please the rain gods. He obeyed. Afterward he roasted the ram and shared it with his neighbors.

Soon rain fell in torrents. Ever since, the legend says, the people of Kingsteignton have roasted a ram at Whitsuntide.

3 Midsummer

In northern Europe people call Midsummer Day "the day that never ends."

For weeks before that day, the sun has been rising earlier each morning and setting later each evening. On Midsummer Day the morning light begins before the evening light has failed. The sky never grows dark. Many people stay up all night to celebrate. They dance around huge bonfires.

Building fires on Midsummer Eve is a

very ancient custom. It began when people were pagans and worshipped a sun god. Then they built bonfires to honor the god.

Those pagan fires were probably built the night before June 21. This is the longest day of the year. But after Christianity came to Europe, people began to celebrate Midsummer Day on June 24. They chose that day because it was the birthday of St. John the Baptist. Now people call their fires either Midsummer Fires or St. John's Fires.

The fires are made in special ways in some places.

In Brittany, in northern France, the wood is piled around a pole decorated with a wreath. The wreath must be placed on the pole by a boy or girl named after St. John. The same boy or girl, named Jean or Jeanne, must also light the fire.

In other parts of France everyone in town must give fuel for the fire. A rich man may give a whole truckload of logs. A poor man may give only a small bundle of sticks. But everyone, even the tiniest baby, must give at least a branch or a twig.

In Belgium the fuel for the fire is gathered by boys and girls who go from house to house singing:

Wood, wood, lumber wood
We come to get St. John's wood.

Along the Danish coast the people build tremendous fires on the beach. Then they row out to sea in boats. From there they watch the double display. They see flames soaring into the sky, and flames reflected in the dark water.

Many people in European countries still believe that Midsummer Fires can do wonderful and magical things.

Norwegian farmers believe that jumping over the fire will bring a good harvest. They say, "As high as you jump over the fire, so high will the grain grow in the coming year."

Portuguese farmers believe that sheep and cattle will be healthier if they are driven through the ashes of a Midsummer Fire.

German sweethearts say that if they leap over a Midsummer Fire together, they will never be parted.

Midsummer Day is an important holiday
for Swiss herdsmen. Every year in April
or May, these men take their flocks up to
high mountain pastures. There the herdsmen
live lonely lives, without their families. But
on Midsummer Day their wives and children
climb up the mountain to visit them. They
all picnic together.

32

The herdsmen have made cheese and
butter for the picnic from the milk of their
cows. Their families have brought ham,
eggs, and Midsummer Bread. This special
kind of bread is made in funny shapes. It
has a flavor a little like licorice.

In some parts of Europe, Midsummer
Day is a special time for young sweethearts.

An old French song says it in this way:

> This is St. John's Day,
> The beautiful day
> When lovers walk together.
> Let us go, Sweetheart.
> The moon is risen.

In Norway, too, Midsummer is a time to think of love and marriage. An old Norwegian folk song has these words:

> They sit among the birches
> In the beautiful Midsummer;
> And before the sun goes down
> They swear faithfulness to each other.

In Sweden, Midsummer Day is the most important holiday of the year, except for Christmas. It is celebrated in city parks, on farms, and in hundreds of villages.

Buildings everywhere are decorated for the day with fresh green birch twigs. The twigs are fastened to house and shop doors.

They are tied to automobiles and buses.

The morning before Midsummer Day, the men and boys of a Swedish village go out into the forest. They cut down a tall straight pine tree. Then they strip off its branches and carry it back to the village green. There they lay it flat on the ground. They call it their maypole, even though the month of May is past.

Women and girls decorate the pole with wreaths and green branches. They fasten a Swedish flag on the top. Usually they put a brightly painted wooden rooster, or other wooden figure, on top of the pole too.

In the afternoon people dress in their best clothes. Some women and girls wear the gay skirts, aprons, and blouses which they save for special occasions. These are native costumes, handed down from mother to daughter for generations.

Everyone gathers at the village green. The maypole is still lying on the ground. The men form lines on both sides of it. A fiddle strikes up an old Swedish tune.

"Heave!" someone shouts.

Up comes the maypole and everyone cheers. When it is upright, the men wedge it into the hole they have dug for it.

The dancing begins. At first even the small children join the grownups in folk dances around the maypole. Later, when the little children have fallen asleep, there is music for modern dancing.

The music goes on all night. The young people dance as if they will never tire.

A girl may gather a bouquet of seven different kinds of flowers on her way home. She puts them under her pillow before she goes to sleep. An old tradition says she will dream of the man she will marry.

4 Harvest Festivals

Harvest time is a time for festivals all over Europe, especially in farming regions. The hard work of bringing in the crops is over. People are ready to enjoy themselves.

In southern Spain farmers and winemakers celebrate the grape harvest. A festival, called the Vintage Fiesta, takes place in the town of Jerez de la Frontera.

After a thanksgiving service in the cathedral, everyone watches the Fiesta parade. Horsemen in Spanish costumes ride prancing horses. Girls wave to the crowd from carriages filled with flowers. Later there are horse races and bullfights. There is lively guitar music for gay singing and dancing.

The German city of Munich holds an Oktoberfest, or October Festival, each year. This city is famous for its beer, which is made from German-grown barley and hops. The festival celebrates the first new beer of the season.

There are displays of farm products at the festival. Folk singers and folk dancers perform. Everyone has plenty to eat and plenty of beer to drink.

Some harvest festivals are in the form of special market days. One takes place in the Swiss city of Bern. The story behind it began in 1405.

That year Bern was almost destroyed by a fire. The town of Fribourg sent a hundred strong men to help rebuild the city. The people of Bern were grateful for the help. They gave Fribourg the right to sell its farm products at a Bern market.

Fribourg had only one important farm product—onions. So, every November since then, an Onion Market is held in the Bern market square. On that day the square overflows with onions. They are piled in wagons and boxes and baskets. They hang in bunches and dangle in strings.

People come from miles around to buy onions and watch the fun. Many wear the native costumes of their villages. Students dressed as onions parade, throwing confetti.

Restaurants serve onion soup, onion-stuffed sausages, onion salad, and even onion cake. Children buy candies shaped like onions.

Another festival with a long history takes place in the English town of Stratford-on-Avon.

It began in the days when servants and farm hands were hired by the year. Their year of work ended after the harvest. Then farmers went to town to hire new workers. Farm hands and servants went to town too, to seek new jobs. They carried their tools to show the kind of work they could do.

The shopkeepers of Stratford-on-Avon held a fair for the people who poured into their town. They set up stalls in the streets to sell food and trinkets. They brought in musicians and dancing bears and other performers. They called it the Mop Fair, for the mops the women servants carried.

42

Today people go to the Mop Fair just to have a good time. They ride on merry-go-rounds. They buy souvenirs. They eat slices of the pig roasted over an open fire by local Boy Scouts.

But today the fair still opens just as it did years ago. An official in a scarlet coat rings a bell. Beside him stands the mayor in a high silk hat and a long black robe.

The mayor welcomes the crowd. He says, "Spend this day of merry-making and frolic so that recollections on the morrow will be without regrets or repinings."

Many European harvest festivals take place on St. Martin's Day, November 11. St. Martin is known as the patron saint of beggars. People used to share their harvest with beggars on this day by giving them a feast.

Now, in some places, children pretend to be beggars on St. Martin's Day. In the Dutch town of Groningen, boys and girls with lighted lanterns beg from door to door. People give them fruit, cake and candy. The children sing silly songs as they walk around. One goes like this:

Here lives a rich man
Who can give us something.
May he live to be very old,
Have a fine death and go to paradise.

Another St. Martin's Day song is:

St. Martin had a cow
That had to go to the butcher.
Whether it was fat or lean,
It had to go to the butcher.
Hooi de booi, hooi de booi!
How beautiful was St. Martin!

Roast goose is a favorite dish for St. Martin's Day feasts. In Sweden, many people

start their meal with a black soup made with prunes and the blood of the goose. They finish with a cake that looks very much like a pile of crisp golden threads. It is made by dripping batter onto a spit turning over a fire.

Not all harvest celebrations take place in the autumn. They can occur whenever a crop is ripe. In Italy, Spain, and southern France, lemons and other citrus fruits ripen all the year around. The French town of Mentone holds its gay Lemon Festival in February.

The decorations for the festival are made of lemons and oranges, grapefruit and tangerines. Fruit covers the arches put up over the main street. Fruit fills the wagons and cars that appear as floats in a parade. Fruit laid out in fancy designs makes a carpet in a city park.

Fishermen too celebrate their harvest—
the harvest they bring up from the sea.
Netherlands fishermen celebrate the first
herring caught each spring.

The excitement begins when the herring
fleets are ready to sail. In each village
people crowd the wharfs to see them off.
The fleets race each other to the fishing
grounds.

The men lower their nets quickly into the sea. They haul them up as soon as they are heavy with fish. The first load of herring brought in by each fleet is put aboard the fleet's fastest boat. Then the boat races to port.

Men waiting at the wharf put the herring into an orange keg. Orange is the official color of the Netherlands. The keg is put into a car decorated with gay streamers. The car roars off toward the royal palace.

The men who reach the palace first, present their fish to the Queen. She thanks them. Everyone in their village is proud of the fleet's victory.

5 Banners, Medals and Giants

Sports contests are a part of many European festivals. In some festivals they are the most important part of all.

The festival called the Gotland Games is really a big sports contest. It takes place on the island of Gotland, off the coast of Sweden. At this festival teams from many villages compete in ten different sports.

The way one team challenges another is part of the fun. One challenge said, "For

800 years you have never been able to beat us at anything. But to amuse ourselves we will let you try again this year."

Among the ten sports of the Gotland Games are wrestling, foot racing, ball games, and hurling contests.

In the sport of *varpa,* men hurl six-pound stones, or metal weights. They throw them at a stake 60 feet away. The winner is the man whose stone or weight lands closest to the stake. The Vikings, who lived on Gotland many centuries ago, probably played this game. Varpa stones, like those used today, have been found in Viking graves.

In the sport of hurling the *caber*, men throw a heavy pole the size of a tree trunk. The caber must turn over once, end for end, before it lands. The winner is the man who throws it the greatest distance.

Hurling is a popular sport in Scotland too. There, a national hurling champion is chosen at a sports festival called the Scottish Games.

In England, Switzerland, Belgium, and Italy men compete in special shooting contests. They use the ancient weapon called a crossbow. The crossbow teams of two Italian towns meet at a festival each summer. The towns, Gubbio and San Sepolcro, have been rivals for centuries.

The teams wear costumes like those worn when armies fought with crossbows. The prize is a magnificent banner. The Italian word for banner, *palio,* gives this festival its name. It takes place in Gubbio and is called the Palio of Gubbio.

Another kind of Palio, or contest for a banner, is held in the ancient Italian town of Siena. There, twice each summer, horses race around the edge of the fan-shaped plaza, or square.

This festival had its beginnings in the days of knighthood. Each horse in the race represents a *contrada,* a section or part of the city. Each contrada has its own costumes, like the clothes worn in the 15th century. Each hires an expert jockey but no contrada owns its own race horse.

All the horses in the Palio are ordinary work animals from farms near the city.

The captains, or leaders of each contrada, draw lots for them. Everybody in Siena hopes his contrada will get the best horse.

On the day before the race, each captain leads his horse to a church. The priest says, "Let this animal receive Thy blessing, O Lord." Then he sprinkles the horse with holy water.

The festival opens with a parade around
the square. There are trumpeters and
drummers. There are men in armor on
horseback. The marchers from each contrada
wear their gay costumes.

Some marchers carry big flags. They
twirl them over their heads and between
their legs. They toss them 30 feet into the
air and catch them behind their backs.

The horses that will race also appear in

54

the parade. So does the palio, or banner,
for the winner. It is in a wagon pulled by
four white oxen. A bell on the wagon clangs
loudly.

When the parade has ended, the horses
line up behind a rope. The jockeys wear
crash helmets and carry whips.

Bang! The starting gun fires. The rope
drops. The horses leap forward. The race
is on.

A Palio jockey is allowed to break all the rules of good sportsmanship. He slashes other jockeys with his whip. He drives other horses into the fence that surrounds the course. Animals crash and fall. Riders fly over their heads.

The wild race ends when the first horse crosses the finish line. He is the winner even if he has lost his jockey.

That evening the contrada of the winning horse is a place of noise and excitement. Everybody celebrates. They have won the Palio!

Knights and noblemen were once the only men allowed to enter the contests that are called ring-tilting tournaments. Today these tournaments, which take place on horseback, are a popular sport of Netherlands farmers. In Denmark, businessmen and housewives ride in them too. Hundreds of riders compete in one famous ring-tilting festival. It is held every July in the Danish town of Sönderborg.

The riders take part in a parade before the tournament. They wear white caps, black coats and boots, and white breeches. They carry long lances tipped with pennants. Boys and girls march ahead of them, or "ride" wooden hobby horses.

Afterward everyone gathers at the tilting
field not far from the center of town. It
is marked off into lanes. A small ring
hangs from a rope or wire stretched across
the end of each lane. The ring is white on
the front and black on the back. The hole
in it is about the size of a quarter.

The riders divide into groups, one group
for each lane. They remove the pennants
from their lances. The tournament begins.

The first rider in each group spurs his horse down the lane at a gallop. He aims his lance at the tiny target that comes closer with each hoofbeat. As he races beneath the ring, he tries to catch it on the point of his lance.

Each player makes 24 "runs" at the ring. Those who spear it every time then take part in the next round. In that round, a rider drops out the first time he misses.

Now the contest becomes more difficult. First each ring is turned around so that its black side faces the rider. This makes it harder to see. Next the rings are replaced by smaller and smaller rings.

One by one the riders miss the ring and drop out. At last only one man and one woman remain out of the hundreds who started. They have earned the titles of king and queen of the tournament.

A very unusual festival contest takes place in the Belgian town of Ath. There, every August, a famous Bible story is acted out. It is "the battle between David and Goliath."

The "David" in the contest is a real person. He is a young man dressed in the white costume of a shepherd.

The "Goliath" is a giant figure fourteen feet high. It is made of reeds and light wood and dressed in armor. A man inside the figure makes it walk and dance and spin around. He sees where he is going through a peephole.

Many Belgian towns have "giants" which they use in all their parades and festivals. They call the figures their "biggest children" and are very proud of them.

David and Goliath parade through the town before the battle. David walks alone, carrying a sling. Goliath carries a club and walks with "Mrs. Goliath." This is another huge figure dressed as a woman. She wears a bridal veil and carries a bridal bouquet.

The parade stops at a church for a ceremony called "The Wedding of Goliath." The two giants "kiss" each other and perform a waltz. Then the parade continues to a big open square.

David and Goliath face each other. A voice from inside the giant makes fun of David, and threatens to destroy him.

David answers, "The right is on my side!"

He puts a stone in his sling. He swings it around over his head and lets the stone fly. As it strikes his enemy he shouts:

"The Evil One is dead!
He has died here,
Having felt the hand of God!"

The crowd cheers, for David has won.

But the people of Ath do not really want their giant to be dead. His battle with David every year is an important part of their lives. So the giant always has the last line in the play.

The voice from inside the big figure shouts it out. "But I'm not dead yet!"

The people cheer again, louder and longer than before. Their contest is over. But they are looking forward to seeing it again the next year, and the year after that.

They know there is one very important thing about every folk festival. It is this: The festival will last as long as people want it to last, even for hundreds and thousands of years.